BASIC INGREDIENTS

THE
POTATO
COOKBOOK

BASIC INGREDIENTS

THE
POTATO
COOKBOOK

MORE THAN SIXTY
EASY, IMAGINATIVE RECIPES

EDITED BY
NICOLA HILL

COURAGE
BOOKS

AN IMPRINT OF
RUNNING PRESS BOOK PUBLISHERS

Philadelphia • London

Canadian representatives:
General Publishing Co., Ltd.,
30 Lesmill Road, Don Mills, Ontario M3B 2T6.

10 9 8 7 6 5 4 3 2
Digit on the right indicates the number of this printing
Library of Congress Cataloguing in Publication Number 94-67592

ISBN 1-56138-492-5
Printed in Singapore

Reprinted 1995

Acknowledgements
Commissioning Editor: Nicola Hill
Editors: Isobel Holland & Jo Lethaby
U.S. Consultant: Jenni Fleetwood
Art Editors: Meryl James & Sue Michniewicz
Production Controller: Sasha Judelson
Jacket Photographer: Nick Carman
Photographer: Alan Newnham
Home Economist: Jennie Shapter
Stylist: Jane McLeish
Illustrators: Roger Kent/Garden Studio and Marc Adams

This edition published in the United States of America in 1995
by Courage Books
an imprint of Running Press Book Publishers
125 South Twenty-Second Street
Philadelphia, PA 19103-4399

Notes
1 pound potatoes yields 3 cups, slices or cubes;
2½ cups small dice or about 2 cups of mashed potatoes.

Microwave methods are based on microwave ovens
with a High Power output of 800 watts.

All the jellies, jams and preserves should be processed in a boiling
water-bath canner according to the U.S.D.A. guidelines.

CONTENTS

The potato must be one of the most widely eaten vegetables in the world, although mostly in just one of its manifestations, the French fry. Despite the disproportionate fame of this single form of preparation, potatoes are one of the most versatile of vegetables and have been a staple in both hemispheres, across the continents and centuries. Not only that, but they can appear in any course of a meal – from appetizers and soups, through to main courses either as an accompaniment or as the main dish, to cakes and desserts.

Although it was, for a time, vilified as being "fattening" and was excluded from the plates of the figure-conscious, a more complete understanding of nutrition has led to the potato being rehabilitated, as long as the temptation to add butter is avoided! Potatoes are not just tasty, they are actually good for you and provide a valuable source of easily digested starch, vitamin C, protein, potassium, iron, thiamin, niacin and dietary fiber, while containing no fat or cholesterol.

History

It is widely known that potatoes were first grown in southern America, but it is astounding just how long a history they have in cultivation. The first archaeological evidence dates back almost 6000 years in areas in the Andes where the potato is part of the native flora.

The first references to potatoes in European writings date from the early sixteenth century, when Spanish conquistadores in South America finally took an interest in things other than gold. Before long, the potato was introduced into cultivation in Spain, Italy, Belgium, Germany and Britain. Within some 50 years they were being widely grown and featured in herbals, albeit in forms rather different to the hybridized cultivars of today. These early forms were, however, mostly collected from tropical areas and grew best in areas where early frosts were unusual, such as the southern parts of continental Europe and the southwest coast of Ireland. Over the years, selections of seedling crosses enabled gardeners to produce varieties that would crop earlier in the year, making them more suitable for colder climates, including the early colonies of North America.

— THE —
POTATO
VARIETIES

HISTORY

There can't be many vegetables that have shaped history, but the course of life in the British Isles and in the U.S. was changed irrevocably by the potato or rather a disease of potatoes.

By the mid-nineteenth century, and for a variety of complex reasons, potatoes had become tremendously important in the diet of the poor in Britain and Ireland. This dependence led to intensive cultivation and this, unsurprisingly with hindsight, created the circumstances in which disease could spread rapidly. The fungus disease, blight, was and still is particularly dramatic in its effects. In 1845 and 1846 crops throughout the British Isles were wiped out by it. The virtual monoculture in Ireland meant that there was nothing to eat there. The results are almost too appaling to contemplate - despite emergency rations and government-run soup kitchens, in 5 years over a million died of starvation and those who could afford to do so emigrated to the U.S. or to England.

Ironically, during the Second World War the potato probably saved many British from starvation once imports of wheat from the U.S. and Canada were reduced to little more than a trickle. The efforts of the Ministry of Food to encourage imaginative use of easily grown root vegetables may seem far-fetched now, but the cartoon character "Potato Pete" had plenty of practical suggestions for livening up the grindingly restricted and monotonous diets of wartime Britain. Once again, the potato played a major role, but this time in supporting life during a time of crisis.

Kennebec

COOKING FOR QUALITY

A renewal of interest in less usual varieties has provided the stimulus to supermarket chains that now supply "heritage" potatoes, albeit at a price, but experimenting with different types needn't be like investing in

Home Guard

the stock-market. Heritage varieties include Home Guard, Maris Peer, Wilja, Golden Wonder, Kerr's Pink, Pink Fir Apple, Romano and Roseval. Simply knowing which is the most suitable type for the culinary purpose you have in mind, and using them accordingly, makes all the difference - good bakers and mashing potatoes, for example, can't be expected to perform well in salads. Keeping in mind a short list of varieties when you go shopping, or looking up any new varieties you come across

increase your knowledge of which potato to buy for your particular needs.

Despite the variety of potatoes available, at least in theory, they can be divided into just two categories according to their cooking qualities - waxy and mealy. Waxy potatoes have a relatively low starch content, but considerable moisture and thin skins. They hold their shape well when boiled or steamed and are excellent cold

Pontiac

in salads or served hot and whole with just a little butter. Mealy potatoes have more starch and become fluffy and light when cooked. They

perform best as bakers for mashing, but may fall apart if boiled too long. This, of course, can be an advantage in thickening soups. Both types can be deep fried.

THE CULTIVATED POTATO

Because they are so readily available and relatively easy to grow, there is a tendency for potatoes to be taken for granted, and perhaps treated with less care and attention than they deserve, both in the kitchen and the garden. Potatoes are often grown on previously uncultivated ground and are considered good ground clearers, because the earthing up involved in growing them

Russet Burbank

has the effect of weeding the ground at the same time. Most varieties, although some more than others, can break up heavy ground and make it easier to grow more temperamental crops, but even a little extra care will improve yields and disease resistance tremendously.

Potatoes are half-hardy plants and both the top growth and tubers can be damaged by low temperature. Equally, however, they need a period of cold for the tubers to become fully dormant and a short day length early in the growing season if the tubers are to develop before the flowering is completed. Special low-chill and day-neutral varieties have been bred for climates where these conditions are not met.

Tremendous efforts have been made by breeders to create plants with resistance to the commonest pests and diseases, including the dreaded blight and now that many of these former scourges are at least under control, there is renewed interest in improving flavor and cooking quality, too. The potato as we now know it is a highly cultivated vegetable, far removed from its wild ancestors. But much of its original variety of flavor and texture has

Maris Peer

certainly been lost in the process. Perhaps new developments in plant breeding can provide the best of both worlds and restore the highly individual qualities of the earlier potato varieties and species in high-yielding, disease-resistant and reliable plants.

Buying and storing potatoes
Although it is tempting and often cheap to buy potatoes in large quantities, resist buying more at a time than you can use in about two to three weeks unless you have ideal storage conditions. Select tubers that are firm and heavy with no soft spots or visible green or black discolored patches. Potatoes that have started to sprout from the eyes should be discarded. The skin of new potatoes should rub away with gentle finger pressure. Ready-washed potatoes store less well than earthy ones.

Store potatoes in cool, dark and dry conditions. Earlies and

Wilja

new potatoes are always better used as soon as possible after lifting and cannot be stored for any length of time, but maincrop potatoes can be kept until the first new potatoes are ready for harvest, with the proviso that any damaged or diseased tubers must be discarded promptly. Below about 45°F the starch content of all types of potato starts to convert to sugar and the flesh blackens. For this reason, they should never be stored in a refrigerator. Exposure to bright light can lead to the flesh turning green which is a sign that a toxin, solanin, which is also present in the leaves and tiny fruits, has developed and the tubers should be discarded.

WHITE OR LIGHT-SKINNED POTATOES
Light in color and with thin skins, these are often found as new potatoes. The flesh may be white or yellow.

Anoka
This is an early variety with round to oval tubers. It is a good general purpose variety and popular for growing in the home garden. The potato flesh remains white after cooking.

Finnish Yellow Wax
As its name suggests, a waxy variety still chiefly found in restaurants and speciality markets. It is ideal for use in salads.

German Fingerling
This is a rather different style of potato, with a cluster of small,

lumpy tubers with yellowish flesh. For a finger potato, the yields are very high.

Green Mountain

This is a medium-late yielding potato with flattened-oblong tubers and dull, creamy skin. The flesh is rather dry and mealy. Introduced in 1878, it is one of many old varieties bred from Rough Purple Chili, along with Triumph, Burbank and Beauty of Hebron.

Irish Cobbler

Was introduced in 1875 but is still widely grown today. It is early to medium-early maturing and produces roundish, smooth-skinned tubers with shallow to deep eyes. The cooking quality is very good and it is moderately disease resistant. It bakes and boils very well.

Katahdin

This potato was introduced in the 1930's, the result of the first systematic attempt at selecting both parents and seedling. It produces mid-season to late tubers, which are elliptical to roundish with smooth, white skin and shallow eyes. The flesh is white. It is a very popular potato, and has some disease resistance.

Kennebec

Provides high yields of mid-season, well-flavored tubers, elliptical to oblong in shape. The cooking quality is excellent and the skin and flesh, which are both white, retain their color well. The very thin skin means that the tubers can be adversely affected by sunlight, so thorough earthing-up is vital. It is resistant to late blight. Illustrated on page 6.

Sebago

Produces late, ivory-yellow, roundish tubers with few and

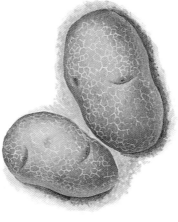

Golden Wonder

shallow eyes. It is resistant to late blight and is widely grown in the South and East in home

gardens. It is less mealy when cooked than Kennebec, but it is still good.

Kerr's Pink

Superior

This is widely grown on the East coast, but its early crop is adversely affected by drought. The tubers are white and oval with smooth to flaky skin. Its dryish white flesh makes excellent French fries.

White Rose

This is a very popular old variety, introduced in 1893 but still widely available. It matures late, producing large, long, flattened elliptical tubers with smooth skin and deepish eyes. The white flesh is perfect for deep frying as it absorbs very little of the oil.

RUSSET OR IDAHO POTATOES
There are the perfect potatoes for baking, slightly dry and fluffy in texture when cooked. They also make excellent French fries and gratins.

Butte
This potato is a typical example of this medium to large variety.

Krantz
This potato is an early russet and fairly disease resistant.

Norgold
It is an early maturing plant with oblong to long tubers, shallow eyes and heavily netted skin. The russeting is uniform and the flesh very white. It bakes and boils well but is susceptible to disease.

Russet Burbank
Also know as Netted Gem, California Russet, Idaho Russet and Golden Russet, is of uncertain original, although perhaps a seedling of Early

Pink Fir Apple

Rose and introduced around 1876. Arguably the most popular variety of all, it is widely grown in Idaho, Maine, Montana, Washington and Oregon, and forms medium-size to large, late maturing plants. The tubers are large, long and cylindrical or slightly flattened with russeted, distinctly netted skin. The numerous eyes are shallow. It is the traditional baking potato but also makes good French fries. Illustrated on page 7.

RED POTATOES
These tend to be fast maturing and can be used small as new potatoes, or left on the plant slightly longer to mature. The skin is very thin and may range in color, depending on variety, from pink to deep red. The flesh is generally white and crisp, and excellent for either boiling or baking.

Red Rose
This is a popular example.

Red La Soda
Identical to La Soda, from which it is derived except for a much more intense red coloration. A medium early, with semi-round to oblong, smooth tubers. The flesh is white and cooks white.

Romano

Norland
Produces a moderate crop of early, somewhat oblong tubers. It has a smooth skin and shallow eyes. The flesh is white and cooks white.

Perfect Peachblow
This potato is also called Red McClure. It was introduced in

Roseval

1880 and has dark red, spherical tubers with few shallow eyes. It performs well on light soils and at high altitudes.

Pontiac
This potato and its darker mutant form Red Pontiac -

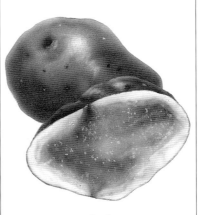

All Blue

are late-maturing varieties with dependable yields but have a tendency to produce oversize tubers. These are round to oblong in shape with deep red skin that may be smooth or flaky. It is easily grown in heavy soil, and is rather susceptible to disease. This potato is resistant to heat and can be stored very well. Its mealy texture makes it ideal for boiling. Illustrated on page 7.

BLUE POTATOES
With their grayish-blue skin and sometimes inky-blue flesh, blue potatoes are still something of a rarity, although a much sought-after one. Their undeniably unusual coloration comes as quite a shock at first, but their delicate flavor should more than compensate. These types of potato lend themselves to the simplest cooking method - simply boil or bake and serve with butter. They are mainly available in speciality markets and some restaurants, but can also be grown successfully in the home garden.

Blue-Carib
This potato is a heritage variety that produces a good crop of large, well-shaped tubers that store well. It is often used for exhibition purposes as its appearance is so pleasing. With its delicate flavor this variety is perhaps best suited to boiling or baking.

All Blue
It has inky-blue skin and flesh, and has an excellent flavor whether boiled or baked.

POTATO & CELERY SOUP

Serves 4

¼ stick butter
½ bunch celery, cut into 1-inch pieces
2 onions, chopped
1 pound potatoes, peeled and quartered
2½ cups chicken or vegetable stock
1 cup milk
½-¾ cup shredded Monterey Jack
or Brick cheese
salt and freshly ground black pepper

Melt the butter in a saucepan, add the celery and onions, and cook gently without browning. Add the potatoes and stock with salt and pepper to taste. Bring to a boil, reduce the heat and simmer for about 20 minutes until all the vegetables are tender.

Purée in a blender or food processor, or rub through a strainer. Return the soup to the rinsed pan. Add the milk, reheat and adjust the seasoning. Serve very hot, sprinkled with the shredded cheese.

MICROWAVE METHOD: Place butter, celery and onion in a casserole dish and cook on High for 3 minutes, stirring twice. Add potatoes and hot stock. Cover and cook on High for 10-12 minutes until potatoes are tender. Purée as above, add milk and cook on High for 2-3 minutes until hot. Season and serve sprinkled with cheese.

CHILLED BASIL & POTATO SOUP

Serves 4

1 tablespoon butter
1½ pounds mealy potatoes, peeled and shredded
6 garlic cloves, halved
1 cup chopped fresh basil
3 cups chicken stock
2½ cups dry white wine
1 teaspoon lemon juice
2 tablespoons ground pignoli (*pine nuts*)
salt and freshly ground black pepper

Melt the butter in a large heavy-bottom saucepan and add the potatoes, garlic and half the basil. Stir over a gentle heat for a couple of minutes, then add the stock and wine.

Bring to a boil and cook uncovered for 15 minutes, until the potatoes are soft. Purée with the remaining basil in a blender or food processor, or rub through a strainer into a bowl. Add lemon juice, salt and pepper to taste, remembering that since the soup is to be served chilled the seasoning will need to be a little more pronounced.

Mix the ground pignoli with 2 tablespoons of the soup in a small bowl. Stir the mixture into the soup. Chill thoroughly before serving.

Illustrated opposite

POTATO & CIDER SOUP

Serves 5-6

2 onions, sliced
1 pound tart apples, peeled, cored and sliced
2 pounds potatoes, peeled and sliced
1¼ cups cider
5 cups vegetable stock
1 teaspoon dried mixed herbs
1 teaspoon ground coriander
⅔ cup plain yogurt
salt and freshly ground black pepper
snipped fresh chives or chopped fresh mint,
for garnish

Combine the onions, apples and potatoes in a saucepan and add the cider. Bring to a boil and cook briskly for 10 minutes, stirring from time to time. Add the stock, dried herbs and coriander. Cover the pan and simmer the soup for about 25 minutes, until all the vegetables are very tender.

Purée the soup in a blender or food processor, or rub through a coarse strainer. Return to the rinsed pan and stir in the yogurt, reserving 1 tablespoon for garnish. Season with salt and pepper and reheat without boiling. Serve with a little yogurt swirled into each bowl and sprinkled with fresh chives or mint.

CORN & POTATO CHOWDER

Serves 4

¼ pound smoked haddock fillets
⅔ cup milk
¼ stick butter
6 bacon slices, diced
1 pound potatoes, peeled and diced
1 large onion, chopped
1 can (*12 ounces*) whole kernel corn
2½ cups chicken stock
⅔ cup light cream
1 tablespoon chopped fresh parsley
salt and freshly ground black pepper

Place the haddock in a saucepan with the milk. Simmer for 10 minutes or until the fish flakes easily when tested with the point of a knife. Remove the fish with a slotted spoon and place on a board. Remove the skin and any remaining bones, flake the fish and set it aside. Reserve the cooking liquid in a pitcher.

Melt the butter in a large saucepan, add the bacon and cook over a moderately high heat until golden. Add the potatoes and onion, cover the pan, reduce the heat and cook slowly until the onion is soft but not browned.

Add the corn, stock, flaked fish and reserved cooking liquid. Simmer gently for 10-15 minutes. Stir in the cream and parsley and season to taste with salt and pepper.

POTATO & TUNA SALAD

Serves 4-6

1 pound salad potatoes, scrubbed
1½ cups flaked canned tuna
½ cup sliced mushrooms
1 red onion, thinly sliced in rings

DRESSING:

½ cup plain yogurt
grated rind and juice of ½ lemon
1 tablespoon chopped fresh parsley
salt and freshly ground black pepper

Cook the potatoes in a saucepan of lightly salted boiling water until just tender. Drain well. Let the potatoes cool, then slice them thickly into a salad bowl.

Add the flaked tuna, sliced mushrooms and red onion rings to the potatoes.

For the dressing, mix the yogurt with the lemon rind and juice. Stir in the chopped parsley with salt and pepper to taste. Pour the dressing over the salad and toss lightly.

NEW POTATO, CHEDDAR CHEESE & CASHEW SALAD

Serves 6-8

1½ pounds new potatoes (*about 16*), scrubbed
6 tablespoons French dressing
4 scallions, sliced,
or 2 tablespoons snipped fresh chives
1 cup finely diced Cheddar cheese
¾ cup salted cashews
12-16 tiny cherry tomatoes
salt and freshly ground black pepper

Cook the potatoes in a saucepan of lightly salted boiling water for about 10-15 minutes until they are all just tender. Drain them and coarsely dice.

Place the potatoes in a bowl and while they are still hot, add the French dressing. Mix well, add the scallions or chives, then cover and leave to cool.

Add the cheese, cashews and cherry tomatoes, season well with salt and pepper and mix lightly. Serve at once or chill in a covered bowl until ready to serve.

CALIFORNIA POTATO SALAD

Serves 4-6

1½ pounds small new potatoes
(*about 18*), scrubbed
6 bacon slices
⅔ cup raisins
¼ cup cashews

DRESSING:

¼ cup plain yogurt
1 teaspoon honey
½ cup crumbled blue cheese
salt and freshly ground black pepper

Boil or steam the new potatoes until tender, about 15-20 minutes, depending upon size. Drain thoroughly, place in a bowl and let cool, if you like.

Cook the bacon until crisp, then crumble or chop coarsely. Mix the bacon with the potatoes and add the raisins.

To make the dressing, mix the yogurt with the honey and cheese in a bowl. Add salt and pepper to taste. Add to the potato mixture and toss well to coat. Serve the salad warm or cold, sprinkled with the cashews.

MICROWAVE METHOD: Place potatoes in a casserole dish with ¼ cup water. Cover and cook on High for 10-12 minutes, until tender. Drain.

POTATO SALAD WITH SALMON & SHRIMP

Serves 4

1¼ pounds waxy potatoes, scrubbed
2 ounces smoked salmon, cut into
thin strips (*½ cup*)
½ pound cooked shelled shrimp
1 cup seedless white grapes, halved
½ cup pecan nuts
1 tablespoon snipped fresh chives
1 tablespoon chopped fresh dill, for garnish

DRESSING:

2 tablespoons mayonnaise
¼ cup sour cream
1 tablespoon lemon juice
salt and freshly ground black pepper

Cook the potatoes in a saucepan of lightly salted boiling water for 15-20 minutes until just tender. Drain well. When cool, slice the potatoes into a salad bowl.

Add the smoked salmon, shrimp, grapes, pecans and snipped chives. Mix the salad lightly, using two forks.

For the dressing, mix all the ingredients in a small bowl. Whisk until thoroughly combined. Pour the dressing over the salad. Toss lightly to coat, sprinkle with dill and serve.

Illustrated opposite

PEANUT POTATO SALAD

Serves 4

1 pound new potatoes, (*about 10*) scrubbed
½ cup diced cooked ham,
¼ cup mayonnaise
1 tablespoon peanut butter
lettuce leaves
½ cup salted peanuts

Boil or steam the new potatoes until tender, about 15-20 minutes, depending upon size. Drain if necessary.

Place the potatoes in a bowl. Add the ham and mix lightly. Mix the mayonnaise and peanut butter together in a small bowl; add to the potato mixture and stir lightly.

Arrange the lettuce leaves on a serving platter and spoon the potato mixture on top. Sprinkle with the salted peanuts.

SPANISH POTATO SALAD

Serves 4

1 pound new potatoes (*about 10*),
scrubbed, or larger potatoes, peeled and
cut into bite-sized pieces
salt
DRESSING:
3 tablespoons tomato paste
3 tablespoons olive oil
1 tablespoon lemon juice
1 garlic clove, crushed
few drops of Tabasco or chili sauce
1-2 tablespoons chopped fresh parsley or
chives, or a mixture of both
salt and freshly ground black pepper

Cook the potatoes in a saucepan of lightly salted boiling water until just tender. Drain. When cool enough to handle, remove the skins if necessary.

Mix the tomato paste with the oil, lemon juice and garlic in a bowl. Add salt, pepper and Tabasco to taste, then stir in the herbs.

Pour the dressing over the potatoes, mix lightly and leave to marinate for 3-4 hours before serving.

POTATO & ZUCCHINI SALAD

Serves 4

1 pound new potatoes (*about 10*), scrubbed
2 cups sliced zucchini
¼ cup corn oil
finely grated rind and juice of 1 small orange
1 tablespoon wine vinegar
1 tablespoon chopped fresh parsley
1 tablespoon snipped fresh chives
or finely chopped scallions
salt and freshly ground black pepper
chopped fresh parsley or snipped fresh chives,
for garnish

Cook the potatoes in a saucepan of lightly salted boiling water until tender. Using a slotted spoon, remove from the water and drain. Add the zucchini to the boiling water, simmer for 5 minutes until tender, then drain.

Put the oil in a bowl with the orange rind and juice, vinegar, parsley and chives or scallions. Season to taste and beat well.

Cut the larger potatoes into halves; leave the small ones whole. Combine the potatoes and zucchini in a bowl, pour on the dressing and toss lightly to mix. The potatoes will absorb the flavor better if they are still warm.

Sprinkle parsley or chives over the salad just before serving. Serve cold.

POTATO SALAD AU VERMOUTH

Serves 6

2 pounds small new potatoes (*about 24*),
scrubbed
⅔ cup chicken stock
¼ cup dry white vermouth
6 tablespoons mayonnaise
3 tablespoons snipped fresh chives,
chopped shallots or scallions
2 tablespoons finely chopped fresh parsley
salt and freshly ground black pepper

Boil or steam the potatoes until tender. Mix the chicken stock and vermouth in a small pitcher.

Peel the hot potatoes and slice them thickly. Put them into a bowl, moistening each layer with stock and vermouth. Set aside until the potatoes are quite cold and have absorbed most of the dressing.

Carefully drain off the excess liquid, if any – it may be used as soup stock. Fold the mayonnaise and herbs carefully into the salad, to avoid breaking the potato slices, and season to taste with salt and pepper. Chill until ready to serve.

HOT POTATOES WITH BACON

Serves 6

**2 pounds small new potatoes
(*about 24*), scrubbed
4 bacon slices
2 tablespoons sesame seeds
2 tablespoons chopped fresh parsley
3 scallions, sliced
DRESSING:
2 tablespoons vinegar
1 teaspoon wholegrain mustard
½ cup corn oil
salt and freshly ground black pepper**

Cook the new potatoes in a saucepan of lightly salted boiling water until tender. Meanwhile, cook the bacon until crisp. Drain the bacon on paper towels and crumble or cut into small pieces.

Spread the sesame seeds on a piece of foil and broil until pale golden. Set aside.

To make the dressing, whisk the vinegar, salt, pepper and mustard together in a salad bowl, then gradually whisk in the oil. Drain the potatoes thoroughly and add to the dressing with the sesame seeds and parsley. Add salt and pepper to taste. Toss together gently. Scatter the bacon and scallions over the salad and serve while still warm.

POTATO & LIMA BEAN SALAD

Serves 6-8

**1½ pounds new potatoes (*about 15*), scrubbed
1 packet (*about ¼ pound*) frozen lima beans
6 tablespoons French dressing
⅔ cup mayonnaise
¾ cup sliced pepperoni
1 bunch scallions, thinly sliced
⅔ cup pitted ripe olives
salt and freshly ground black pepper**

Cook the potatoes in a saucepan of salted boiling water for about 10-15 minutes until they are just tender. Drain well. Cook the lima beans in a saucepan of lightly salted boiling water until just tender. Drain.

Cut the warm potatoes into quarters and place in a bowl. Combine the dressing and the mayonnaise in a pitcher and season well. Pour over the potatoes and toss until coated.

Add the lima beans, pepperoni, scallions and olives; toss again. Spoon the salad into a bowl. Cover and chill in the refrigerator until ready to serve.

Illustrated opposite

DAUPHINE POTATOES

Serves 6

1½ pounds mealy floury potatoes, peeled
1 egg yolk
pinch of ground nutmeg
corn oil, for deep-frying
salt and freshly ground black pepper

CHOUX PASTRY:

7 tablespoons water
½ stick butter
pinch of salt
¾ cup all-purpose flour
2 eggs

To make the choux pastry, heat the water, butter and salt in a saucepan. Bring to a boil, add the flour all at once and beat to a smooth paste. Cook for 1 minute. Remove from the heat and gradually beat in the eggs to make a smooth glossy paste.

Cook the potatoes in a saucepan of lightly salted boiling water until just tender. Drain well and press through a strainer to purée them. Beat in the egg yolk and nutmeg and season to taste. Mix with the choux paste and leave to cool.

Heat the oil to 350°F, or until a cube of bread browns in 1 minute. Drop spoonfuls of the potato mixture into the oil and cook until golden. Drain and serve at once.

SAUTEED POTATOES WITH GARLIC

Serves 4-6

1½ pounds potatoes, peeled and cut
into 1-inch cubes
3 tablespoons olive oil
3 large garlic cloves, peeled
salt
finely chopped fresh parsley, for garnish

Rinse the potato cubes in a colander and dry thoroughly with paper towels.

In a large, deep skillet that will take the potatoes in a single layer, heat the oil. Cook the garlic cloves slowly until they are just golden. Add the potatoes and sauté, tossing constantly, over moderate heat for 5 minutes, or until browned on all sides. Sprinkle the potatoes with salt. Half-cover the pan with a lid or foil and cook the potatoes very slowly, shaking the pan and turning them occasionally, for about 15 minutes, or until they are crisp and golden on all sides and feel soft inside when pierced with a fork or skewer.

Remove potato cubes from pan with a slotted spoon. Discard garlic cloves. Drain potatoes thoroughly and serve immediately, sprinkled with more salt and garnished with parsley.

Note: It is important not to pierce the garlic cloves, and vital that they do not burn, otherwise they will impart a bitter taste.

CAPE POTATO PUDDING

Serves 4-6

2 pounds mature Idaho potatoes, peeled
½ stick butter or margarine
3 tablespoons milk
1 teaspoon sugar
3 eggs, beaten
1 teaspoon finely grated lemon rind
salt

Cook the potatoes in a saucepan of lightly salted boiling water until tender. Drain. Melt half the butter in a large saucepan with the milk. Add the potatoes. Mash them, then beat well until smooth. Add the sugar and slowly work in the beaten eggs and lemon rind. Add salt to taste.

Use a little of the remaining butter to grease a 5-cup soufflé dish. Spoon the mixture into the dish and dot the surface with the remaining butter.

Bake in a preheated oven, 375°F, for 25-30 minutes until lightly browned. Serve the "pudding" immediately as an accompaniment to fish with a sauce, or with roast or broiled meats.

POTATO & GREEN PEPPER RATATOUILLE

Serves 4

2 tablespoons corn oil
½ pound potatoes, sliced
1 onion, sliced
1 sweet green pepper, cored, seeded and sliced
1 sweet yellow pepper, cored, seeded and sliced
1½ pounds plum tomatoes,
peeled and chopped
1 tablespoon soy sauce
2 tablespoons tomato paste
salt and freshly ground black pepper

Heat the oil in a saucepan and sauté the potatoes, onion and peppers for 5-10 minutes.

Add the tomatoes, soy sauce, tomato paste and salt and pepper to taste. Bring to a boil, cover and simmer for 40 minutes or until the vegetables are tender. Serve hot.

Illustrated on pages 2-3

BAKED POTATOES

Serves 4

4 large baking potatoes, scrubbed and dried
salt
freshly ground black pepper
BACON & MUSHROOM FILLING:
4 bacon slices
½ stick butter
1 cup chopped chestnut or button mushrooms
SHRIMP & SCALLION TOPPING:
1½ cups cooked shelled baby shrimp
⅔ cup sour cream
⅔ cup plain yogurt
a few drops of Tabasco sauce
4 scallions, finely chopped
SALMON & SOUR CREAM TOPPING:
½ pound cold poached salmon
or 1½ cups drained canned salmon
1¼ cups sour cream
1 teaspoon lemon juice
2 teaspoons chopped fresh thyme,
or ½ teaspoon dried
¼ cup slivered almonds, toasted, for garnish

Prick the potatoes all over with a fork and rub with salt. Wrap each potato in individual pieces of foil if liked. Bake in a preheated oven, 400°F, for 1-1½ hours or until tender. Alternatively, double-wrap the potatoes in heavy-duty foil and place in the hot coals of a preheated barbecue. Bake for about 45 minutes, turning frequently.

Once cooked, remove the potatoes from the foil, if used and prepare as follows. (Each filling is sufficient for four large potatoes.)

For the bacon and mushroom filling, cut a slice lengthwise from the top of each baked potato and scoop out the flesh. Cook the bacon until crisp, drain on paper towels and crumble. Mix with the mashed potato flesh and half the butter. Melt the remaining butter in a skillet, add the mushrooms and sauté for about 3 minutes. Remove from the heat and stir the mushrooms into the bacon and potato mixture, season to taste with salt and pepper. Return the mixture to the potato skins and return the potatoes to the oven or place on the oiled grill of the barbecue. Cook for about 10 minutes until heated through.

For the shrimp and scallion topping, cut the baked potatoes almost in half lengthwise and crosswise to form a criss-cross. Combine the filling ingredients, season to taste and heap onto the potatoes.

For the salmon and sour cream topping, cut a deep criss-cross as above in the baked potatoes. Flake the poached or canned salmon, removing any skin and bones. Mix with the remaining topping ingredients and season to taste. Pile the mixture on top of the baked potatoes and garnish with the slivered almonds.

Illustrated opposite

POTATO, LEMON & THYME CASSEROLE

Serves 4-6

1½ pounds potatoes, peeled
5 tablespoons olive oil
1 large onion, sliced
2 tablespoons lemon juice
1 teaspoon grated lemon rind
⅔ cup chicken stock
1 tablespoon chopped fresh thyme
salt and freshly ground black pepper

Cut the peeled potatoes into slices about ½-inch thick, and then halve each slice. Wash the slices and pat them dry.

Heat 3 tablespoons of the olive oil in a deep skillet; add the sliced onions and cook until they start to brown. Add the prepared potatoes and the remaining oil and continue cooking over a moderate heat, stirring, until the onions and potatoes turn lightly golden.

Add the lemon juice, lemon rind, stock and thyme, with salt and pepper to taste. Cover and cook slowly, stirring from time to time, for 25-30 minutes, by which time the water should have evaporated and the potatoes will be sitting in a richly flavored oil. Serve hot.

PAN HAGGERTY

Serves 6

2 tablespoons olive oil
2 large onions, thinly sliced
1½ pounds potatoes, peeled
¼ stick butter
1 cup shredded Cheddar cheese
salt and freshly ground black pepper

Heat the olive oil in a large skillet, add the onions and cook over a low heat until soft and transparent. Remove from the pan.

Cut the potatoes into ⅛-inch slices and pat them dry on paper towels.

Melt the butter in the skillet. Arrange the potatoes, onions and cheese in layers in the skillet, reserving a little cheese for the top. Begin and end with potato slices. Season each layer with salt and pepper.

Cover the pan and cook over a low heat for 30 minutes, or until the vegetables are tender. Sprinkle the remaining cheese over the top and brown under a preheated hot broiler for a few minutes. Serve at once.

POTATO &
HAZELNUT BAKE

Serves 4

1¼ pounds potatoes, peeled
1 small onion, finely chopped
2 tablespoons chopped fresh parsley
3 tablespoons chopped hazelnuts
⅔ cup chicken stock
⅔ cup milk
2 eggs, beaten
⅓ cup shredded Swiss cheese
salt and freshly ground black pepper

Slice the potatoes very thinly with a sharp knife, a mandolin or the slicing blade of a food processor. Layer the potato slices with the onion, parsley, 2 tablespoons of the chopped hazelnuts, and salt and pepper to taste, in a greased deep ovenproof dish.

Mix the stock with the milk and eggs in a bowl. Add salt and pepper to taste. Pour the mixture over the potatoes and sprinkle with the remaining hazelnuts. Cover the dish with foil and bake in a preheated oven, 375°F, for 40 minutes (hand-sliced potatoes will be slightly thicker, and will take longer to cook).

Remove the foil and sprinkle with the grated cheese. Bake for a further 15-20 minutes, until the potatoes are golden and tender.

CHEESE
CROQUETTES

Serves 4

2 cups mashed potato
1½ cups thinly shredded Gruyère, Stilton
or Cheddar cheese
1 egg yolk
3 tablespoons all-purpose flour
1 egg, beaten
2½ cups fresh bread crumbs
1 tablespoon freshly grated Parmesan cheese
corn oil, for cooking
salt and freshly ground black pepper

Mix the potato with the cheese. Beat in the egg yolk and season to taste with salt and plenty of pepper. Shape the mixture into 16 croquettes. Roll the croquettes in the flour, dip them in the beaten egg and finally coat them thoroughly in a mixture of bread crumbs and Parmesan. Arrange in a single layer on a plate and chill until ready to use.

Heat oil to a depth of ½-inch in a skillet and cook the croquettes over a medium heat for about 5-10 minutes, turning constantly so they cook evenly. When the croquettes are golden brown and crisp, remove them from the pan and drain on paper towels.

POTATO CHIPS

Serves 4

4 potatoes, peeled
corn oil, for deep-frying
salt

Thinly slice the potatoes crosswise with a sharp knife, a mandolin or the slicing blade of a food processor. Soak the slices in ice water for 15-20 minutes to remove the excess starch and to crisp the potatoes. Drain the potato slices and dry them thoroughly on a clean cloth or paper towels.

Heat the oil for deep-frying to 375°F, or until a cube of bread browns in 30 seconds. Place a few potato slices in the frying basket and lower into the fat. Cook for 3-5 minutes until the chips are golden brown, turning if necessary. Remove the basket and drain the chips on a cloth or paper towel. Repeat with the remaining potato slices. Serve the potato chips in a bowl, sprinkled with salt.

POTATO SKINS WITH SOUR CREAM DIP

Serves 5-10

5 large baking potatoes, scrubbed and dried
⅔ cup sour cream
1 teaspoon snipped fresh chives
corn oil, for cooking
salt and freshly ground black pepper
snipped fresh chives, for garnish

Prick the potatoes with a fork. Bake directly on the shelves of a preheated oven, 400°F, for about 1¼ hours until tender.

Meanwhile, prepare the dip. In a bowl, mix the sour cream with the chives. Season to taste. Cover the bowl and leave to chill.

When the potatoes are cooked, cool for a few minutes and cut each one into quarters lengthwise. Scoop out most of the potato flesh, leaving a thin layer next to the skin. (The scooped-out potato may be used to top a pie.)

Pour the oil into a small deep skillet to a depth of 3 inches. Heat the oil to 375°F, or until a cube of bread browns in 30 seconds. Add the potato skins carefully to the hot oil. Cook for about 2 minutes until brown and crisp. Remove, drain on paper towels. To serve, arrange on a plate with the dip, sprinkled with chives, in the center.

Illustrated opposite

LEEK, POTATO & CORIANDER BAKE

Serves 4

2 tablespoons corn oil
¼ stick butter
1 pound leeks, trimmed, washed
and cut into ¾-inch rings
2 pounds small waxy potatoes,
such as Finnish Yellow Wax, scrubbed
and cut into ½-inch slices
1 teaspoon black peppercorns
2 teaspoons coriander seeds
1 teaspoon salt

Put the oil and butter in a large shallow roasting pan and place in a preheated oven, 400°F, until the butter is just melted. Add the prepared leeks and potatoes, turning them over several times to coat them with the oil and butter. Level the mixture in the pan.

Crush the peppercorns with the coriander seeds. (If you have no pestle and mortar, put the seeds and peppercorns between two double sheets of nonstick brown paper or waxed paper and crush with a rolling pin.) Tip the mixture into a bowl and stir in the salt. Sprinkle the spice mixture over the vegetables and mix lightly. Cook for 45-50 minutes or until the potatoes are nicely browned.

POTATO HERB BISCUITS

Makes 8

¾ pound potatoes, peeled
1 tablespoon butter
2 tablespoons snipped fresh chives
2 tablespoons chopped fresh parsley
¾ cup all-purpose or whole wheat flour
a little milk (*optional*)
corn oil, for cooking
salt and freshly ground black pepper

Cook potatoes in a saucepan of lightly salted boiling water for 15-20 minutes until tender. Drain. Put the potatoes in a bowl and mash with the butter. Add salt and pepper to taste and stir in the chives and parsley. Beat in the flour. Add a little milk if the mixture is dry.

Form the potato mixture into a ball and knead lightly until it is smooth and free from cracks. Roll out on a lightly floured board to a thickness of ¼-inch. Prick the surface all over with a fork and then cut into neat triangle shapes.

Lightly oil a heavy-bottom skillet, heat and cook the potato triangles, a few at a time, for 3 minutes on each side until golden brown.

POTATOES BRAISED IN RED WINE

Serves 4

1½ pounds potatoes, peeled and
cut into ¼-inch slices
1¼ cups dry red wine
2 tablespoons chopped fresh thyme
2 tablespoons chopped fresh parsley
salt and freshly ground black pepper

Place the potato slices in a casserole dish or ovenproof dish and pour in the red wine. Sprinkle with the chopped fresh herbs and salt and pepper to taste. Mix lightly so that all the potatoes are coated with wine and herbs.

Cover the casserole dish or ovenproof dish with a lid or foil. Bake in a preheated oven, 375°F, for about 1 hour, or until the potatoes are tender and almost all the wine has been absorbed. Stir twice during cooking. The potatoes will be a delicate pink color on the outside but still white inside. Serve hot.

EGGPLANT & POTATO CASSEROLE

Serves 4

2 eggplant, thinly sliced
1 pound potatoes, peeled and thinly sliced
1 small onion, grated
1 cup shredded Swiss cheese
⅔ cup chicken or vegetable stock
1 tablespoon corn oil
salt and freshly ground black pepper

Spread out the eggplant slices in a colander and sprinkle them liberally with salt. Leave for at least 30 minutes, then wash the slices and drain well.

In an ovenproof casserole dish arrange layers of the potato and eggplant slices, sprinkling each layer with a little of the grated onion, cheese and salt and pepper. Arrange the top layer so that there are alternating slices of potato and eggplant overlapping in a circle.

Pour in the chicken or vegetable stock and brush the top layer with the oil. Cover the casserole dish with foil and bake in a preheated oven, 375°F, for about 30 minutes. Remove the foil and cook for 30-45 minutes or until the vegetables are tender and the top is brown.

POTATOES DAUPHINOISE

Serves 4-6

**1½-2 pounds evenly-shaped potatoes,
peeled and thinly sliced
1 garlic clove, peeled and halved
butter, for greasing
1 teaspoon freshly grated nutmeg
1¼ cups light cream
¾ cup shredded Swiss cheese
salt and freshly ground black pepper**

Cook the potatoes in a saucepan of lightly salted boiling water for 5 minutes. Drain and cool slightly.

Rub the cut garlic clove around the inside of a deep ovenproof dish. Grease the dish with plenty of butter. Arrange the potatoes in layers, sprinkling each layer with nutmeg and salt and pepper.

Pour the cream over the potatoes. Sprinkle the shredded cheese over the surface so that the potatoes are completely covered. Cook, covered, in the center of a preheated oven, 350°F, for about 1-1¼ hours, or until the potatoes are cooked through and the cheese topping is crusty and golden brown, uncovering the dish after 45 minutes.

Illustrated on pages 2-3

FANTAIL POTATOES

Serves 4-8

**8 baking potatoes, about ½ pound each,
peeled and halved lengthwise
¼ cup olive oil
8 garlic cloves, unpeeled
10-12 thyme sprigs
salt**

Place the potatoes cut-side down. Using a sharp knife make cuts at ¼-inch intervals along the length of each potato almost through to the base, just leaving a hinge to hold them together.

Heat the oil in a roasting pan in a preheated oven, 400°F, until hot. Add the potatoes to the pan and spoon the oil evenly over each one. Roast the potatoes for 30 minutes. Baste well and sprinkle with a little salt, if you like.

Add the garlic and thyme and cook for a further 30 minutes or so until the potatoes are golden brown and crisp; the cuts will open out a little to create the fantail shape from which the recipe takes its name.

Illustrated opposite

ROSTI

Serves 4

2 pounds even-sized mealy potatoes, scrubbed
¾ stick butter
1 small mild onion, very finely chopped
salt and freshly ground black pepper

Cook the potatoes in a saucepan of lightly salted boiling water for about 7 minutes. Drain. When the potatoes are quite cold, peel them and shred them coarsely into a bowl.

Heat 1 tablespoon of the butter in a large, heavy-bottom skillet. Add the onion and cook for about 5 minutes until soft. Stir into the potato and season.

Melt the remaining butter in the skillet. Set aside about 1 tablespoon of the melted butter in a cup. Add the potato mixture to the pan and form into a neat cake. Cook gently, shaking the pan occasionally so that the rösti cake does not stick, for about 15 minutes longer, or until the underside of the cake is a crusty golden brown. To cook the top, pour over the reserved melted butter and either place under a preheated broiler to brown, or turn in the pan and brown. To serve, invert the rösti cake onto a flat heated dish and cut it into wedges.

Illustrated on page 1

HERB-BAKED NEW POTATOES

Serves 4

1½ new potatoes (*about 16*), scrubbed
salt
freshly ground black pepper
4 mint sprigs
4 parsley sprigs
FOR GARNISH:
1 tablespoon chopped fresh mint
1 tablespoon chopped fresh parsley

Grease a sheet of foil large enough to enclose the potatoes. Put the potatoes into the center and sprinkle them with the salt and pepper. Tuck the mint and parsley sprigs among the potatoes. Fold the foil around the potatoes and seal the edges.

Bake the potatoes in a preheated oven, 400°F, for 40-45 minutes, until they are tender.

Remove the potatoes from the foil and place them in a serving dish. Sprinkle with the chopped mint and parsley and serve.

SOUFFLE CHEESE POTATOES

Serves 4

4 baking potatoes, scrubbed and dried
1½ tablespoons butter
½ cup small curd cottage cheese
2 tablespoons freshly grated Parmesan cheese
2 teaspoons Dijon or wholegrain mustard
2 eggs, separated
salt and freshly ground black pepper

Prick the potatoes with a fork. Place on a baking sheet and bake in a preheated oven, 375°F, for about 1¼ hours, until tender.

Cut a lengthwise slice from the top of each potato; carefully scoop most of the potato flesh into a bowl, leaving a shell.

Mash the potato flesh with the butter. Add the cottage cheese, 1 tablespoon of Parmesan, the mustard and the egg yolks. Stir in salt and pepper to taste.

Whisk the egg whites in a grease-free bowl until stiff but not dry; fold lightly into the potato mixture. Spoon into the potato shells, then sprinkle with the remaining Parmesan.

Return the potatoes to the oven for a further 15-20 minutes, until well risen, golden and puffed. Serve immediately.

NEW POTATOES WITH FENNEL & MINT

Serves 6

2 pounds tiny new potatoes (*about 24*), scrubbed
1 tablespoon butter
1 small fennel bulb, trimmed and finely chopped
2 tablespoons chopped fresh mint
salt and freshly ground black pepper
mint sprigs, for garnish

Cook the potatoes in a saucepan of lightly salted boiling water until just tender. Drain.

Put the butter into the warm pan and heat gently. Add the fennel and cook for about 5 minutes until just beginning to brown. Season well with pepper.

Tip the cooked potatoes into the pan, add the chopped mint and toss the potatoes so that they are coated with butter, mint and fennel. Serve hot, garnished with sprigs of mint.

off

35

NEW POTATO CURRY

Serves 4

2-inch piece of fresh ginger, minced
2 garlic cloves, crushed
¼ cup clarified butter or ½ stick butter
2 large onions, finely chopped
2 bay leaves
1 stick cinnamon, broken into short lengths
2 teaspoons fennel seeds
3 green cardamoms
1 teaspoon turmeric
2 pounds small new potatoes
(*about 24*), scrubbed
2½ cups water
1¼ cups plain yogurt
salt and freshly ground black pepper

FOR GARNISH:

chili powder
chopped fresh cilantro leaves

Mix the minced ginger and crushed garlic together in a small bowl.

Place the clarified butter or stick butter in a large saucepan or wok and heat. Add the chopped onions, the ginger mixture, bay leaves, broken cinnamon stick, fennel seeds, cardamoms and turmeric to the melted fat. Cook the mixture gently, stirring constantly, until the onion is soft but not browned.

Add the scrubbed potatoes to the saucepan or wok, pour in the measured water and season with salt and pepper to taste. Bring the mixture to a boil, lower the heat and cover.

Simmer the curry steadily for 10 minutes, then uncover the pan and cook fairly rapidly for a further 10 minutes, or until most of the water has evaporated.

Pour the plain yogurt over the potatoes and heat through fairly gently to avoid curdling the sauce.

Transfer the curry to a serving dish and sprinkle with chili powder to taste and chopped fresh cilantro before serving.

MICROWAVE METHOD: Place the clarified butter or stick butter, ginger, crushed garlic, chopped onion, bay leaves, cinnamon, fennel, cardamom and turmeric in a large casserole dish. Cook on High for 3 minutes, stirring twice. Add potatoes and ⅔ cup water. Cover and cook on High for 15 minutes, or until the potatoes are tender. Stir in ⅔ cup yogurt and then serve as above.

Illustrated opposite

POTATO &
CAULIFLOWER
CURRY

Serves 6-8

**1 pound potatoes, peeled and
cut into 1-inch pieces
1 large cauliflower, separated into
small flowerets, thick stem discarded
6 tablespoons clarified butter or ¾ stick butter
1 onion, finely chopped
2 garlic cloves, finely chopped
2-inch piece of fresh ginger,
peeled and minced
2 teaspoons ground coriander
1 teaspoon dried onion flakes
1 teaspoon turmeric
1 teaspoon chili powder
3 tablespoons tomato paste
2 teaspoons garam masala
salt and freshly ground black pepper**

Cook the potato chunks and cauliflower flowerets in separate saucepans of lightly salted boiling water until the vegetables just begin to soften. Drain the potato and cauliflower, reserving the cauliflower water.

Meanwhile, heat the clarified butter or butter in a heavy-bottom saucepan. Add the chopped onion and garlic to the pan and cook for 3 minutes. Stir in the minced ginger and cook gently for 2-3 minutes. Add the ground coriander and dried onion flakes, if using, and cook for a further 30 seconds. Add the turmeric, chili powder and 1 teaspoon each of freshly ground black pepper and salt. Stir well and cook for a further 2 minutes. Stir the tomato paste into the mixture.

Add the cooked potato and cauliflower to the saucepan with ⅔ cup of the cauliflower water and toss gently in the spice mixture. If the curry becomes too dry, add a little more of the reserved cauliflower water.

Cook for 5-6 minutes, then sprinkle in the garam masala and cook for a further minute. Serve the curry hot with boiled rice and a selection of accompaniments.

EGGPLANT & POTATO CURRY

Serves 4

¾ **pound eggplant, cubed**
2 teaspoons salt
3 tablespoons corn oil
½**-1 teaspoon chili powder**
1 teaspoon turmeric
2 teaspoons ground cumin
2 teaspoons ground coriander
1-inch piece of fresh ginger,
peeled and minced
¾ **pound potatoes, peeled and cubed**
1 can (*8 ounces*) tomatoes
2 tablespoons lemon juice
2 tablespoons chopped fresh cilantro leaves
1 teaspoon garam masala

Place the eggplant in a colander, sprinkle with 1 teaspoon of the salt and set aside for 20 minutes. Rinse under cold water and drain.

Heat the oil in a saucepan, add the chili powder, turmeric, ground cumin, coriander and ginger and cook over a gentle heat for 2 minutes. Add the potatoes and drained eggplant and cook, stirring, for 2 minutes.

Add the canned tomatoes, lemon juice, chopped fresh cilantro and remaining salt. Cover and simmer for 25 minutes or until the vegetables are tender. Just before serving, stir in the garam masala.

POTATO STICKS

Serves 5-6 as a snack

1½ **pounds potatoes**
corn oil, for deep-frying
2 tablespoons garam masala
2 teaspoons salt
½**-2 teaspoons chili powder (*optional*)**

Slice two potatoes at a time into very thin matchsticks, using a sharp knife – do not prepare more than two potatoes at a time, or they will discolor.

Heat the oil for deep-frying to 375°F, or until a cube of bread browns in 30 seconds. Immediately add the potato matchsticks and cook for 3-5 minutes, or until golden.

Lift the sticks out of the oil, drain and place on paper towels to remove excess oil. Repeat the process until all the potatoes have been used. Sprinkle with garam masala, salt and chili powder to taste, if using. Serve the sticks immediately, while hot.

POTATO SAMOSAS

Makes 40

DOUGH:

4 cups all-purpose flour
½ teaspoon baking powder
1 teaspoon salt
¼ stick butter, melted
¼ cup plain yogurt
about ½ cup warm water

FILLING:

½ stick butter
2 small onions, finely chopped
5 cups finely diced cooked potatoes
½-1 fresh green chili, seeded
and finely chopped
2 teaspoons garam masala
1 tablespoon shredded coconut
corn oil, for deep-frying
salt and freshly ground black pepper

Sift the flour with the baking powder and salt into a mixing bowl. Make a well in the center and add the melted butter and yogurt. Draw the flour into the liquid, using a wooden spoon, adding water as necessary to make a smooth dough. Knead until free from cracks and set aside.

To make the filling, melt the butter in a large skillet, add the onion and cook over a gentle heat for 5 minutes until soft and lightly colored, then add the potatoes and chilies and sauté the potatoes until golden brown, turning frequently. Add the garam masala and coconut, and season with salt. Stir well to mix and leave to cool.

On a lightly floured board or work surface roll 20 balls of dough the size of a shelled walnut into thin circles, 6-inches in diameter. Cut each circle in half. Shape each semi-circle into a cone and fill with a little of the potato mixture. Dampen the top edges with water and press together firmly to seal.

Heat the oil for deep-frying to 375°F, or until a cube of bread browns in 30 seconds. Deep-fry the samosas, a few at a time, until golden brown all over. Drain the samosas on paper towels and serve hot, sprinkled with freshly ground black pepper.

Illustrated opposite

POTATO PANCAKES

Serves 4-6

1 pound potatoes, peeled
¼ cup very hot milk
½ cup all-purpose flour
4 eggs, beaten
½ teaspoon dried mixed herbs
¼ cup heavy cream
corn oil, for cooking
salt and freshly ground black pepper
parsley sprig, for garnish

Cook the potatoes in a saucepan of lightly salted boiling water until tender. Drain well, then mash until very smooth. Beat in the boiling milk and leave to cool completely.

Using a wooden spoon, beat in the flour and eggs. Stir in the herbs and cream, and season with salt and pepper. Beat until very smooth – the mixture should resemble a thick batter.

Heat the oil in a large skillet and swirl it around. When the oil begins to give off a slight haze, drop in tablespoons of the batter, a little apart, and cook for 2 minutes on each side, until golden brown.

Place the pancakes in layers in a clean dry dish towel and keep warm in a preheated oven, 275°F. Repeat with the remaining batter. Serve the pancakes very hot, garnished with parsley.

SPANISH OMELET

Serves 4-6

½ cup olive oil
1 pound potatoes, peeled and
chopped or sliced
2 onions, chopped
1 sweet red pepper, cored, seeded and chopped
or cut into strips
1 sweet green pepper, cored, seeded and
chopped or cut into strips
2-3 garlic cloves, crushed or finely chopped
2 cups chopped, peeled tomatoes
6 eggs
salt

Heat ⅓ cup of the oil in a large saucepan, add the potatoes and cook over a low heat, turning frequently, for about 15 minutes.

Meanwhile, heat the remaining oil in a large nonstick skillet. Add the onions and peppers, and sauté over a low heat for about 8-10 minutes. Just before the vegetables are cooked, add the garlic, tomatoes and cooked potatoes. Mix lightly.

Beat the eggs in a bowl with a little salt. Pour the mixture evenly over the vegetables and cook, over a low heat, until the egg has just set. Turn the omelet out on to a large plate, serve and cut into wedges.

PUMPKIN & POTATO PIE

Serves 6-8

1 pound pumpkin, peeled,
seeded and cubed (*about 3 cups*)
½ stick butter
1 large onion, sliced
¾ pound potatoes, scrubbed
1 package (*1 pound*) frozen puff pastry, thawed
1 egg, beaten
salt and freshly ground black pepper

Place the pumpkin cubes in a saucepan with water to cover. Add a large pinch of salt. Bring to a boil, then lower the heat and cook gently until soft – about 15 minutes. Drain very thoroughly, then return the pumpkin cubes to the saucepan.

Meanwhile, melt the butter in a skillet, add the sliced onion and cook gently until soft and golden brown. Add to the pumpkin, stirring well to mix.

Cook the potatoes in a saucepan of lightly salted boiling water until almost tender. Drain and let cool slightly. Peel the potatoes and cut them into ½-inch cubes. Stir the cubed potato into the pumpkin mixture, with salt and pepper to taste.

Roll the pastry out thinly and cut out two circles – one measuring 10-inches in diameter, the other 12-inches in diameter. Place the smaller circle on a greased baking sheet. Spread the pumpkin filling over the pastry, leaving a ½-inch edge of pastry around the outside of the circle and piling the filling in the center.

Brush the pastry edge with beaten egg, then place the second circle of pastry on top. Press well to seal and scallop the edges with a knife. Any remaining pastry scraps can be cut into shapes to decorate the top.

Chill the pie for 15 minutes, then brush it with the rest of the beaten egg. Place the pie in a preheated oven, 425°F, and bake for about 15 minutes, then reduce the heat to 375°F, and bake for a further 15 minutes, until the pastry is crisp and brown.

Transfer the pie to a serving plate, cut into wedges and serve hot.

GNOCCHI DI PATATE

Serves 3-4

1½ pounds mealy potatoes, peeled
¼ stick butter
1 egg, lightly beaten
½ teaspoon baking powder
1½ cups all-purpose flour
½ cup melted butter
6 tablespoons freshly grated Parmesan cheese
2 tablespoons fine dry bread crumbs
salt and freshly ground black pepper
salad leaves, for garnish

TOMATO SAUCE:

1 can (*about 14 ounces*) chopped tomatoes
3 tablespoons tomato paste
½ teaspoon dried oregano

Cook potatoes in lightly salted boiling water until just tender. Drain well and mash to a purée with butter. Beat in the egg and baking powder, seasoning generously with salt.

Start adding the flour to the potato purée, a handful at a time, working it in smoothly with your fingers. As the purée stiffens, transfer it to a board dusted with more of the flour. Continue kneading in as much of the remaining flour as is needed to make a manageable dough – it may not be necessary to use it all. Divide the dough into four parts and let them "rest" for about 10 minutes.

Meanwhile, put a large saucepan of lightly salted water on to boil. Have a kettle of water simmering in readiness and the broiler hot, with four individual baking dishes warming underneath it.

To make the gnocchi, shape a portion of the dough into a cylinder measuring roughly ½ -¾-inches in diameter. Cut it into 1 inch lengths. Alternatively, shape the dough into a solid triangular "roll," about 1½ inches along each side. Cut this into ½ inch wide slices. Repeat with the remaining dough.

Place the tomato sauce ingredients in a small saucepan and heat gently. Bring to a boil and simmer for 5 minutes. Season to taste.

Drop the gnocchi into the saucepan of boiling water. They will first sink to the bottom and then float to the surface. Once they have done so, simmer them for 3 minutes. With a slotted spoon, transfer the gnocchi to a colander. Rinse them with boiling water and drain well.

Pour 1 tablespoon of the melted butter into each hot baking dish. Using all of the gnocchi and tomato sauce, layer the gnocchi and sauce in each dish. Sprinkle with the remaining butter, the Parmesan and the bread crumbs. Place the dishes back under the broiler to brown and crisp the tops. Sprinkle with black pepper and serve hot with a salad garnish.

Illustrated opposite

POTATO & SAUSAGE BRAID

Serves 4-6

DOUGH:

1½ cups all-purpose flour
½ teaspoon salt
¾ stick margarine
½ cup mashed potato, strained
beaten egg, to glaze

FILLING:

1 pound sweet sausage meat
4 tablespoons pickle or chutney
1½ cups sliced cooked potatoes
½ cup shredded Cheddar cheese
salt and freshly ground black pepper

To make the potato dough sift the flour and salt together into a large mixing bowl. Cut in the margarine and rub gently with your fingertips until the mixture resembles fine bread crumbs. Then work in the strained mashed potato to make a firm dough.

Place the dough on a lightly floured surface, and roll out to a 12-inch square. Carefully place the dough on a baking sheet and mark into three pieces lengthwise.

Season the sausage meat with salt and pepper and spread it down the center section of the pastry. Cover the sausage with the pickle or chutney then lay the slices of cooked potato and shredded cheese on top.

Make a series of diagonal cuts in the pastry 1 inch apart on either side of the sausage meat, to within ½ inch of the filling. Brush the strips with water and bring them to the center, braiding them over the sausage filling. Press the ends together to seal and trim.

Brush the braid with the beaten egg and bake in a preheated oven, 425°F, for 15 minutes, then reduce the heat to 400°F, and bake for a further 25-30 minutes. Serve hot with a selection of vegetables, or cold with a salad.

ALMOND POTATOES

Serves 4

¾ pound potatoes, cooked
and mashed with milk and butter
(*about 1½ cups*)
seasoned flour, for coating
1 egg, beaten
1 cup almonds, finely chopped
¼ stick butter
1 tablespoon corn oil
salt and freshly ground black pepper
parsley sprigs, for garnish

Divide the mashed potato into 12 pieces. Place the flour on a plate. Shape each potato piece into a medallion shape, coating it with flour as you do so. Dip each medallion in the beaten egg and then the almonds.

Heat the butter and oil in a large skillet and cook the medallions, a few at a time, for about 6 minutes, turning once, until golden. Drain on paper towels. Serve hot, garnished with sprigs of parsley.

STIR-FRIED POTATOES

Serves 4

1 pound potatoes, shredded
and rinsed to extract the starch
3 tablespoons corn oil
2 cups finely chopped vegetables, such as onion,
cauliflower, sweet peppers, green beans,
broccoli, celery, zucchini, parsnip, mushrooms,
cabbage, leeks, and corn
2 tablespoons soy sauce
1-inch piece of fresh ginger, minced
salt and freshly ground black pepper

Use a cloth to squeeze the excess moisture from the shredded potato. Heat the oil in a large nonstick pan or wok. Cook the shredded potato for 5-10 minutes or until nearly cooked, stirring frequently.

Add the chosen vegetables, soy sauce, ginger and salt and pepper and stir-fry briskly for a further 5-10 minutes to cook the vegetables yet still keeping them crisp. Serve hot.

LANCASHIRE HOTPOT

Serves 6

3 tablespoons corn oil
2 pounds lean neck of lamb (*with bones*),
cut into chunks and
tossed in 3 tablespoons seasoned flour
2 lambs' kidneys, cored and sliced
4 onions, finely sliced
1½ cups diced carrots
1½ pounds potatoes, scrubbed and sliced
1 bay leaf
½ teaspoon dried marjoram
½ teaspoon dried thyme
2 cups chicken stock
salt and freshly ground black pepper

Heat 2 tablespoons oil in a skillet and brown the flour-coated meat chunks, a few at a time. Lightly brown the kidneys. Layer the lamb, onions, kidneys, carrots and potatoes in a large casserole dish, seasoning each layer lightly with herbs, salt and pepper. Finish with a layer of potato slices.

Heat the stock in the skillet then pour into the casserole dish. Brush the potatoes with the remaining oil. Cover the dish and cook in a preheated oven, 325°F, for 2 hours, until the meat is tender. Remove the lid, increase the heat to 400°F, and cook for a further 30 minutes to brown the potatoes.

PORK BAKE

Serves 4-6

4 bacon slices, chopped
1 large onion, chopped
1 cup quartered mushrooms
1 teaspoon chopped fresh sage,
or ½ teaspoon dried
1 teaspoon chopped fresh thyme,
or ½ teaspoon dried
1 pound lean pork, cubed and
tossed in 2 tablespoons seasoned flour
1 pound potatoes, peeled and sliced
1¼ cups chicken stock
¼ stick butter, cut into flakes
salt and freshly ground black pepper

Cook bacon in a skillet for 3 minutes. Add onion and cook until soft. Add mushrooms, herbs and seasoning and cook for 1 minute. Remove mixture using a slotted spoon and set aside. Add pork to pan and brown. Add the bacon mixture.

Put one-third of mixture into the bottom of a casserole dish. Cover with a layer of potatoes. Repeat layering twice more. Pour over the stock. Dot top layer of potatoes with butter. Cover the casserole dish. Bake in a preheated oven, 350°F, for 1½ hours, remove lid and bake for 15 minutes more, to brown the potato topping.

Illustrated opposite

BAKED CHICKEN

Serves 4-6

¾ stick butter
**8 chicken breast fillets, halved and
tossed in ½ cup seasoned flour**
2 pounds potatoes, peeled and thinly sliced
1 large onion, thinly sliced
2½ cups chicken stock
salt and freshly ground black pepper

Melt half of the butter in a Dutch oven. Add the flour-coated chicken pieces and brown for 10 minutes, turning. Transfer the pieces to a plate. Remove casserole dish from the heat.

Arrange one-third of the potato slices in the casserole dish. Melt the remaining butter and brush one-third over the potatoes and season. Arrange half the onion slices on the potatoes. Place 8 of the chicken pieces on the onions. Arrange half the remaining potato slices over the chicken pieces. Brush with half the remaining melted butter, then season. Repeat the onion, chicken and potato layers. Brush with the remaining butter, then season.

Pour the stock over to just cover the potatoes. Cover with greased parchment paper and the casserole lid. Cook in a preheated oven, 300°F, for 2 hours. Uncover the casserole dish, increase heat to 375°F, and cook for 30 minutes more.

CORSICAN CHICKEN

Serves 6

**12 Canadian bacon slices
cut into large cubes**
3-pound broiler-fryer chicken
¼ stick butter
2 cups small button mushrooms
3 garlic cloves, crushed
**1 teaspoon chopped fresh basil,
or ½ teaspoon dried**
1 can (*about 14 ounces*) chopped tomatoes
¾ cup chicken stock
⅓ cup pitted ripe olives
1 pound small new potatoes (*about 12*), scraped
2 tablespoons brandy
salt and freshly ground black pepper

Heat the bacon in a flameproof casserole dish over a gentle heat until the fat runs. Raise the heat, cook the bacon until crisp, then remove. Add the chicken and butter to the casserole dish. Brown the chicken on all sides. Add the mushrooms, garlic and basil, seasoning to taste. Cover the casserole dish and cook in a preheated oven, 375°F, for 30 minutes.

Add the canned tomatoes, bacon, stock, olives, potatoes and brandy. Stir well, cover and cook for a further 30 minutes. Remove the lid and cook for 30 minutes more. Remove the chicken from the casserole dish and carve into six pieces. Spoon the sauce over the chicken and serve.

CHICKEN & HOT PEPPER POTATO GOUGERE

Serves 4

1 pound potatoes, peeled
1 tablespoon butter
¼ cup water
⅓ cup all-purpose flour
1 egg, beaten
½ cup crumbled Stilton, Gorgonzola
or other blue cheese

FILLING:

¼ stick butter
1 small onion, finely chopped
1 sweet red pepper, cored, seeded and diced,
or ½ x 11 ounce jar whole sweet red
peppers in brine, drained and diced
3 tablespoons all-purpose flour
⅔ cup chicken stock
⅔ cup milk
1 pound cooked chicken,
cut into bite-size pieces
salt and freshly ground black pepper

Cook the potatoes in a saucepan of lightly salted boiling water until tender. Drain very thoroughly, then return to the empty pan and dry over a low heat for 1-2 minutes. Press the potatoes through a strainer into a bowl or mash them thoroughly.

Put the butter into a small pan with the water and a generous pinch of salt. Heat until the butter has melted, then bring to a boil. Quickly tip in the flour all at once and beat well until the mixture leaves the sides of the pan. Gradually beat in the egg, then beat this mixture into the mashed potato, adding the blue cheese and mix well. Thoroughly grease a large oval baking dish and place spoonfuls of the mixture around the outer edge of the dish.

To make the filling, melt the butter in a saucepan, add the chopped onion and fresh pepper, if using, and sauté over a gentle heat for 4-5 minutes until soft. Stir in the flour and cook for 1 minute. Gradually add the stock and milk, stirring until the mixture boils and thickens. Lower the heat and simmer for 3-4 minutes. Season, then stir in the chicken and drained peppers in brine, if using.

Spoon the filling into the center of the gougère. Bake in a preheated oven, 425°F, for 20-25 minutes until crisp and golden.

51

SUMMERTIME SHRIMP POTATOES

Serves 4

2 pounds small new potatoes,
(*about 24*), scrubbed
2½ cups chicken stock
1½ cups diced cooked ham
1 pound cooked shelled shrimp
1 tablespoon white wine vinegar
2 teaspoons chopped fresh mint
2 tablespoons chopped fresh parsley
4 scallions, finely chopped
salt and freshly ground black pepper

Cook the potatoes in the boiling stock in a saucepan until just tender. Meanwhile, mix the ham with the shrimp in a bowl. As soon as the potatoes are cooked, remove them from the pan, using a slotted spoon, and set aside.

Bring the stock to a boil in the open pan and boil rapidly until it is reduced by half. Add the vinegar, ham and shrimp. Return the potatoes to the pan and heat through gently for 1 minute, then add the herbs and scallions. Stir well to combine all the ingredients, taste and adjust the seasoning if necessary, adding salt and pepper to taste. Serve immediately with brown bread and a green salad.

BAKED RED SNAPPER WITH POTATOES & OLIVES

Serves 4

1 pound potatoes, peeled
and very thinly sliced
2 lemons, sliced
¾ stick butter
1 large or 4 small red snapper, cleaned
1 cup pitted ripe and green olives
olive oil, for sprinkling
salt and freshly ground black pepper
dill sprigs, for garnish

Arrange the sliced potatoes and lemons in a layer in the bottom of a large greased shallow baking dish or roasting pan and dot generously with butter.

Place the fish on top of the potatoes. Season with salt and pepper and scatter the olives over the snapper. Sprinkle the fish generously with olive oil and bake in a preheated oven, 375°F, for 30-40 minutes depending on the size of the fish, or until the flesh flakes easily and is tender. Serve at once, sprinkled with sprigs of dill.

Illustrated opposite

PAN-FRIED BUBBLY WITH SARDINES

Serves 4

1½ pounds potatoes,
cooked and mashed (*about 3 cups*)
1 egg, beaten
1 small onion, minced
3 tablespoons corn oil
1 large sweet green pepper
1 can (*about 8 ounces*) tomatoes
1 tablespoon tomato paste
½ teaspoon dried mixed herbs
8 fresh sardines, cleaned
½ cup shredded Cheddar cheese
salt and freshly ground black pepper
1 tablespoon chopped fresh parsley, for garnish

Combine the mashed potato, beaten egg and minced onion together in a large bowl. Add salt and pepper to taste.

Heat the oil in a large skillet with a flameproof handle, add the potato mixture and smooth with a knife or spatula. Gently cook in the oil for 10-15 minutes until golden brown underneath.

Meanwhile, scorch the skin of the green pepper under a hot broiler. Transfer the pepper to a bowl and cover with several layers of paper towels. When cold, peel the skin off the pepper, then cut the pepper lengthwise into strips. Set aside.

Mix the canned tomatoes, tomato paste and dried mixed herbs together in a small saucepan and heat gently. Pour the tomato mixture over the potatoes in the skillet. On top of this form a wheel shape with the sardines, with their heads pointing outward, and arrange strips of green pepper between each sardine.

Position the skillet under a preheated broiler, and broil the bubbly under a moderate heat for 6-8 minutes, or until the sardines are cooked. Sprinkle the shredded Cheddar cheese over the top, increase the heat and broil until the top is golden and bubbling.

Garnish the bubbly with the chopped parsley and cut into wedges. Serve at once.

JANSSON'S TEMPTATION

Serves 4-6

8 potatoes, cut into ¼ inch thick strips
2 onions, finely chopped
2 cans (*2 ounces each*) anchovy fillets
1 cup light cream
¼ stick butter
1 cup fresh bread crumbs
freshly ground black pepper

Arrange the potatoes, onions and anchovy fillets in a greased ovenproof dish, with a layer of potatoes as the topping. Season the cream with pepper. Pour over the potatoes. Melt the butter, mix with the bread crumbs and sprinkle over the top of the potatoes.

Bake in the center of a preheated oven, 375°F, for 1¼ hours until the potatoes are soft.

MICROWAVE METHOD: Layer potatoes, onions and anchovies as above. Pour over seasoned cream. Cover and cook on High for 18-20 minutes, or until potatoes are tender. Place butter in a small dish and cook on High for 30-45 seconds to melt. Mix with bread crumbs and sprinkle over potatoes. Place under a preheated broiler to brown.

CRAB CAKES

Serves 4

1 onion, finely chopped
½ cup chopped mushrooms,
½ stick butter or margarine
½ cup all-purpose flour
⅔ cup milk
1 teaspoon Worcestershire sauce
2 tablespoons chopped parsley
½ pound fresh, canned or frozen crabmeat
½ pound cooked mature potatoes, mashed without any additional liquid (*about 1 cup*)
2 eggs, beaten
¾-1 cup dry bread crumbs
4 tablespoons corn oil, or ½ stick butter
salt and freshly ground black pepper

Gently cook the onion and mushrooms in the butter, until soft. Add ¼ cup of the flour and stir over a low heat for 2-3 minutes. Blend in the milk and stir as the liquid comes to a boil and thickens. Season lightly and add the Worcestershire sauce, parsley and crabmeat.

Blend the mashed potatoes with the crab meat mixture. Chill until firm enough to form into eight round cakes.

Season the remaining flour and use to coat the crab cakes. Brush them with beaten egg, then roll in the bread crumbs. Heat the oil or butter in a large skillet and cook the cakes until crisp and brown on both sides.

POTATO BREAD

Makes a 2 pound loaf or 16 rolls

2 cups white bread flour
2 cups whole wheat flour
1 package rapid-rise active dry yeast
2 teaspoons salt
½ cup mashed potato, sieved
1 cup warm water
milk, to glaze

Mix the flours, yeast and salt in a bowl and rub in the mashed potato. Add the warm water and mix to a soft dough. Transfer to a floured surface and knead for 10 minutes until smooth and elastic.

Shape the dough and place in a greased 9 x 5-inch loaf pan. Cover with waxed paper and leave to rise in a warm place for about 45-60 minutes until doubled in bulk. Alternatively, shape the dough into 16 rolls and arrange on greased baking sheets; cover and leave to rise for 25 minutes.

Brush the surface of the loaf or rolls with milk. Bake in a preheated oven, 450°F, for 30-40 minutes until the bread is well risen and sounds hollow when tapped underneath. Remove the loaf from the pan and cool on a wire rack. Rolls will only require 15 minutes baking.

ROQUEFORT BREAD

Makes a 1 pound loaf

4 cups white bread flour
2 teaspoons salt
¼ stick butter
1 package rapid-rise active dry yeast
⅔ cup lukewarm milk
1 cup sieved cooked potato
1 cup crumbled Roquefort or blue cheese
beaten egg, to glaze

Sift the flour with the salt into a warmed bowl. Cut in the butter; rub in until the mixture resembles fine bread crumbs. Stir in the yeast. Stir the milk into the sieved potato in a bowl, then work this mixture into the flour to make a soft but not sticky dough. Knead on a floured board for 5 minutes, then knead in the crumbled cheese.

Grease a 7 x 3-inch loaf pan. Shape the dough to fit the pan, or shape into a round cob shape and place on a greased baking sheet. Cover with waxed paper and leave to rise in a warm place for 30 minutes, or until the loaf has doubled in bulk. Brush the loaf with beaten egg and bake in a preheated oven, 400°F, for 15 minutes. Reduce the heat to 350°F, and bake for 15 minutes more. Remove the loaf from the pan, if using, and leave to cool on a wire rack.

Illustrated opposite

CHOCOLATE PUDDING WITH CHOCOLATE SAUCE

Serves 4

1 stick butter
½ cup sugar
2 eggs, beaten
¼ cup unsweetened cocoa powder
1 teaspoon baking powder
½ cup sieved cooked potato
½ cup ground almonds

CHOCOLATE SAUCE:

⅔ cup light cream
**4 squares (*4 ounces*) semisweet
chocolate, grated**

Cream the butter and sugar together in a large mixing bowl until light and fluffy. Gradually beat in the eggs, beating well after each addition.

Sift the cocoa powder and baking powder together and gently fold into the mixture, then fold in the sieved cooked potato and the ground almonds.

Spoon the mixture into a greased 4-cup pudding mold. Cover the mold with a circle of waxed paper and then with a circle of foil which has been pleated to allow room for the pudding to rise. Secure the paper covering securely with kitchen string.

Steam the chocolate pudding on a trivet or upturned saucer in a saucepan half-filled with boiling water for 1½ hours – adding more boiling water to the pan as necessary. When the pudding is cooked, remove the pudding mold from the saucepan and let stand for 5 minutes.

Meanwhile, to make the chocolate sauce, bring the light cream to a boil in a small saucepan, then remove from the heat. Add the chocolate, stirring until it has melted and the sauce is smooth.

Invert the pudding out on a heated dish and serve it immediately, with the hot chocolate sauce poured over.

NECTARINE CHEESE PIE

Serves 6

¾ **cup self-rising flour**
¼ **cup ground hazelnuts**
½ **teaspoon apple-pie spice**
½ **stick butter**
½ **cup mashed potato**
⅓ **cup sugar**
1 **egg, lightly beaten**
½ **cup cream cheese, softened**
½ **teaspoon vanilla extract**
3 **nectarines, halved and pitted**

Place the flour, ground hazelnuts and apple-pie spice together in a large bowl. Mix well together then cut in the butter; rub in with your fingertips. Stir in the mashed potato and ¼ cup of the sugar and knead lightly until the mixture forms a dough.

Lightly grease an 8-inch loose-based fluted pie pan and press the dough into the prepared pan with floured fingertips. Press the dough well into the sides and prick well all over with a fork.

Place the pie shell in the center of a preheated oven, 375°F, and bake for 25-30 minutes until lightly browned. Remove the pie shell from the oven and reduce the temperature to 350°F.

Meanwhile, place the beaten egg, softened cheese, vanilla and remaining sugar in a bowl and mix together.

Place the nectarine halves on a work surface. Using a sharp knife cut each half into ¼ inch slices, keeping the slices together at the base.

Arrange 5 of the nectarine halves around the edge of the cooked pie shell and one in the center of the pie, slightly fanning out the slices. Carefully spoon the soft cheese mixture over the nectarines to cover all of the fruit and the pie shell.

Return the pie to the oven and bake for 30-35 minutes until the filling is set and lightly golden. Carefully ease the pie out of the pan and serve warm with cream.

FARMHOUSE FRUITCAKE

Serves 10-12

¾ cup tub margarine
1 cup firmly packed brown sugar
½ cup sieved mashed potato
1 tablespoon light corn syrup
1 cup all-purpose flour
1 cup whole wheat flour
1 tablespoon baking powder
1 teaspoon apple-pie spice
3 eggs, beaten
⅔ cup golden raisins
½ cup chopped almonds
½ cup candied cherries, quartered
soft brown sugar, for sprinkling

Place the margarine and brown sugar in a mixing bowl and cream together until pale and fluffy. Beat in the mashed potato and corn syrup.

In a second bowl, mix together the all-purpose and whole wheat flour, the baking powder and the spice. Gradually beat the eggs into the creamed potato mixture, a little at a time, adding some of the flour mixture if necessary to prevent curdling.

Fold into the remainder of the flour the mixture, together with the golden raisins, chopped almonds and candied cherries.

Line and grease an 8-inch deep cake pan. Spoon the cake batter into the prepared pan and sprinkle the top with brown sugar.

Place the cake in the center of a preheated oven, 300°F, and bake for 2½ hours, or until the cake has risen and is firm to the touch.

Leave the cake in the pan for 5 minutes, then invert on a wire rack, remove the lining paper and let cool. Serve the farmhouse fruitcake cut into wedges.

Illustrated opposite

POTATO GINGERBREAD

Makes 12-15 slices

1¼ cups all-purpose flour
1 teaspoon baking powder
1 teaspoon apple-pie spice
1 teaspoon ground ginger
pinch of salt
½ cup shredded raw potato
¼ cup candied cherries, chopped
⅓ cup golden raisins
⅓ cup light corn syrup
½ stick butter
1 egg, beaten
1 teaspoon baking soda
1 tablespoon water

Sift the flour, baking powder, apple-pie spice, ground ginger and salt into a mixing bowl. Stir in the shredded potato, candied cherries and golden raisins and mix well.

Melt the syrup and butter in a small saucepan, let cool slightly, then add to the dry ingredients with the egg. Mix the baking soda with the water and add to the mixture. Beat well.

Spoon the mixture into a greased and lined 9 x 5-inch loaf pan. Bake in a preheated oven, 350°F, for 40 minutes, or until the gingerbread feels firm to the touch. Invert on a wire rack to cool.

DATE & NUT LOAF

Makes 12-15 slices

1½ cups chopped dates,
½ cup chopped walnuts
¼ stick margarine
1 teaspoon baking soda
⅔ cup firmly packed brown sugar
¾ cup boiling water
1 egg, beaten
2 cups self-rising flour
½ cup sieved mashed potato

Place the chopped dates, chopped walnuts, margarine, baking soda and brown sugar in a bowl. Pour over the boiling water, mix well and allow to cool. Stir in the beaten egg, flour and sieved mashed potato and beat well with a wooden spoon.

Spoon into a greased and lined 9 x 5-inch loaf pan and bake in a preheated oven, 350°F, for 1 hour. Cover the loaf with foil and bake for a further 15-20 minutes until firm.

Invert on a wire rack and let cool. Serve sliced, with butter.

APRICOT & GOLDEN RAISIN BISCUITS

Makes 12

1 cup all-purpose flour
1 tablespoon baking powder
½ teaspoon salt
½ teaspoon ground cinnamon
½ stick butter
½ cup mashed potato
2 tablespoons sugar
3 tablespoons golden raisins
¼ cup dried apricots, chopped
1 egg, lightly beaten

Sift the flour, baking powder, salt and ground cinnamon into a bowl. Cut and rub in the butter and mix in the mashed potato. Stir in the sugar, golden raisins and dried apricots.

Add about half of the beaten egg and mix lightly to form a soft dough. Tip the dough out onto a floured surface and roll out to about ¼-inch thick. Cut it into 12 rounds with a 2-inch cutter.

Place the rounds on a baking sheet, brush with the remaining egg and bake in a preheated oven, 425°F, for 10-12 minutes until the biscuits are brown and well risen.

Cool on a wire rack. Serve split and buttered.

RUM TRUFFLES

Makes 20

8 squares (*8 ounces*) semisweet chocolate, coarsely grated
½ cup mashed potato
1⅓ cups confectioners' sugar, sifted
1 tablespoon rum,
or a few drops of rum extract
chocolate sprinkles

Melt the chocolate in a heatproof bowl over a saucepan of hot water, then gradually beat the chocolate into the mashed potato in a bowl. Cover and let stand until cold, then beat in the confectioners' sugar and the rum or rum extract. Refrigerate until firm.

Roll the mixture into balls about the size of a walnut. Dip the balls into the chocolate sprinkles and place in small paper candy cups. Store in the refrigerator until required – they are ideal served with coffee after dinner.

—THE—
POTATO
INDEX